CHARADES AND CELEBRATIONS

✳✳✳ *CHARADES AND CELEBRATIONS*

poems by Constance Urdang

OCTOBER HOUSE INC. *New York*

Some of these poems have appeared in *Burning Deck, Carleton Miscellany, Chelsea, Chicago Review, The Paris Review, Perspective, Poetry, Poetry Northwest, The Quarterly Review of Literature, The Sewanee Review, The Texas Quarterly.*

Published by October House Inc.
55 West Thirteenth Street, New York

Copyright © 1965 by Constance Urdang
All rights reserved
Library of Congress catalog card number 64-13165
Printed by Clarke & Way, Inc., New York, U.S.A.
First Edition

For my father (1889-1960) and mother

Contents

ONE

Five Celebrations

1. *The Invitation*

'The honour of your presence' has been requested
In a world of aunts, nuclear warheads and vitamin pills.

Grandma, in spangles, can levitate to the ceiling
Quicker than you would suppose—and the dancing bear,

That's Grandpa, darling, the claws are a practical joke.
Your sister the moon will be there, and the fireflies will sing

In the cool of the afternoon. The invitations
Have been sent out, engraved and illuminated;

'To meet' the aunts: that stout one with the cigar,
Another one skinny, a third in a violet toque;

How puzzling are the gifts and messengers
Of love, that come in such grotesque disguises.

2. *Birth*

Mother said she found me curled in a banana leaf;
It was morning of course; the sun with inquisitive yellow
Fingers poked into my secret—which was simply

To be born. In the odor of ripeness a single
Scorpion has already swooned to death
Where the yellow indifferent fingers of the fruit

Point up from the mysterious dust. Mother said
She slept, afterwards, and the breeze blew hothouse airs
Over my cradle in the banana leaf.

3. *An Evening of Home Movies*

When Aunt Insomnia came back from the planet Mars
With two hundred color slides, five anecdotes,
Some postcards with pretty views of the universe,

And an extra suitcase filled with souvenirs,
Who could imagine her spin, like a top, through space,
And end over end, besides, in her rayon chemise,

Hand-knitted cardigan, and elasticized hose?
It must have filled the angels with tenderness.
She has travelled faster and farther than you would suppose,

To look at her. Has she forgotten the marvels she saw
(The comets with dragon-tails, the siren-stars,
And earth, that was home, a will-o'-the-wisp below)?

Give thanks for her safe return from wherever she goes.
She has shown us the way. Let us listen and be wise,
Say thank you politely, and treasure the souvenirs.

4. *Death*

At the death of the little black cat
The universe closed like a clam.

The stars sang, 'O how beautiful he was,
How black he was, and his paws dipped in milk, how white;
His eyes were bottomless, deserted and green as the water in a
    quarry.'

The verdict was murder in the case of the little black cat
Although the lightning found no one to accuse.

How long did he lie there in the moon-colored road
Before the moon took him? Pale moon-cat goddess Pasht,
Tearer and render, devourer of darkness who holds
The sun in your eyes through the gloom of the under-world,
Console us for the death of the little black cat.

The road spills white as milk to the black edge
Of the world, in the mouse-colored morning. The universe
Shuddered shut like a clam at the death of the little black cat.

5. *The Query*

Right now on the flat roof of the world
A man is selling balloons; he pulls them out
Of the sky; meanwhile, of course, a band

Is playing, four shoeshine boys make change, and
Somebody is running to catch a bus. What
Does it have to do with us? Even there the flowers

Do not bloom 'in perpetuity'; they are renewed
Quietly, by the municipal authorities. The musicians belong
To a union, and the man with the balloons

Would like to live in Chicago and get rich.
However, the message written along the sky
By the fountains is not all lies;

I'll read it for you: it says, Right now
On the flat roof of the world, three hundred balloons
Like a cluster of grapes, ripen in the bright blue garden.

The Old Woman

Sister, my unborn sister, somewhere inside
Me, lives an old woman, bones of a wren,
Hide tough as tanned leather to hold her together,
Beach-grass hair on an eggshell head.
Her nest is in an old coat. Without a shadow
She walks, fastidious as a crab that leaves no footprints.

How shall I know her? All up and down the streets
I have looked for her among the leaves blowing;
In the neighborhood store I have hidden myself among groceries
To catch her when she comes in on her errand;
None of the faces is hers, in the lighted bus.

Sister, old woman, don't hide in your wintry weather:
I have swallowed the moon like you. I mean no harm.
You know my magic. The same tide
That pulls, at the full, in my blood, is at ebb in you.
Together we walk, one cat in the grey of the alley.

Shadow, my mother's daughter, when one day I see
Your face in my mirror, will you recognize me?

The Eleven Sorrows

Being, first, the sorrow of birth
    which is leaving home for the first time

Second, the sorrow of love
    because it is so soon forgotten

The sorrow of rain in the street
    which strums on germination and decay

Next, the sorrow of the acorn
    which foresees nothing

Then, the sorrow of youth
    which is called Impatience

The sorrow of pleasures past
    to be sounded on the trombone, a mournful instrument

Consider the sorrow of the fields in winter
    for Persephone is an undutiful daughter

The sorrow of flowers in a vase
    for they have gone under the knife

The sorrow of old men
    which is the odor of loneliness

The sorrow of old women
    for they have arrayed themselves as a bride

Lastly, the sorrow of a bad death
    that we may be spared the wound that suppurates and
    is never healed, for no green seedling can sprout there

The Fairy Tale

The same old story
Of the little lost children
Sent to the forest
Because of love:

The mother-ogre
Who locked the door
Blew out the candle.
Bird will steal,

Squirrel will snatch,
Fish will gobble,
Ant will carry off
The crumbs in the pocket.

Deep in the thicket,
Look down, look down
Stones, cold stones
Will lead them home.

There are twelve versions,
The first by a lady
Who thought it was pretty
The second told

By the littlest boy
When he grew old
To his own grand-daughter;
The third is in Latin.

And so on, until
All over the world
Scholars can find it.
Squirrel on the branch,

Duck on the pond,
Fish in the river,
Ant in the dust,
Children in the forest,

Who has solved
The riddle behind it?
Love drove them out,
Love called them home;

Bread betrayed them,
Stones fed them;
The mothers that carried them
Tell them this story.

Memory and Prophecy

1.

Through a field of real buttercups
An imaginary child runs; the time is always past;
The child is myself; someone imagined me
In the middle distance, among brilliant flowers.

2.

What shall I see in the mirror, mother,
When I am old?

A round rough hill without a track,
Chicory, columbine, fleabane, mullein stalk,
Flick of a grouse in the tangled brush,
Two black steers come to lick salt.

Editorials

for G. A. (1880–1918)

No. 1

This angel is wearing a
Crash helmet   His teeth
Are bared but he is not
Smiling   No   His gleaming teeth
Are red white and blue   This angel
Is an American   Yes
When he re-enters the atmosphere
You and I will crumble to ash and be dispersed
Imperceptibly over the surface
Of the slowly-spinning globe which is
After all neither American nor
Un-American

No. 2

It is time for the Others
To come up out of the earth   the
Worms slugs and dark crawlers even
Ouroboros the perfect zero, encompassing
All of nothing within the closed circle
Of himself   Dark ones
Are you ready to come and do battle
With these swords of light   There is too much light
How it dazzles splinters pierces spits us   Say it, the light
Has made us blind

No. 3

Ah furniture
Chairs tables sofas lamps rugs and curtains
Philodendrons
Art needlework
Swedish modern headboards, conversation pits
Electric rotisseries, washing machines
How lyrical you are

No. 4

He is still outsmarting them playing
Hide-and-go-seek   (they think
He does not exist because they
Have not found him)   Ha-ha
What is the cry of the abominable snowman
Ha-ha-ha   He has invented
In the capacious interior of his enormous
Brain-case   (larger
Than man's)   a cloak of invisibility and
Bear-tracks to lead us
Ha-ha up the mountain path
O beautiful secret beast
Your existence is an abomination because
You refuse to let us offend you

Four Charades

'It is not exactly beauty that I mean. It is that the thing is in itself enough.'

—*Letter of Virginia Woolf to V. Sackville-West*

To arrive on earth carrying one's own luggage

Pure invention: the sky I have caused to appear at the end
    of the street;
Perfection of raindrops; ice; incorruptible nature. Myself
I invented first: hands, feet, hat, shoes, mother,
Daughter and son. Little caterpillar,
Will you marry me when you become a butterfly?

The poor, and the children of the poor, being the little sparrows

To go back to the earth like them, being old.
To make discoveries among the ants and at the foot
Of a grass-blade tall as a tree, to find
Comfort in a crumb and solace in the tiny landscape
Of worm-casts, sticks, pebbles, broken glass and dandelions;
To see what is smallest, without patronizing,
To consider the gravity of the question,
Where shall I set my next footprint.

Mr. North Wind, I have come to call for your daughter

Across the untroubled water, color of salmon,
The faintest music calls, saying, Come, come,
Tinged with the darkness that wells up from under the sea,
Wreathed with the streamers of darkness that blow from the pure
Circle of the horizon, the twilight girls

Might dance where the sandpipers, curlews, terns, gulls and
      gannets have left
On the wet, opalescent sand prints of their spidery feet.

If the pulse of the Atlantic can be heard beating in St. Louis

Three times the same airliner has crossed the same window,
The barely perceived curve of its trajectory tracing the curve
      of the sky,
Wide, pale, and hazy with high clouds.
                                  Tumbling birds below
Chase the wind and each other above the wind-troubled leaves.
The turbulence up there is invisible;
Possibly it does not exist. Sky full of wind,
Let the birds rest, when night comes, under your stars.

Promise to an Unborn Child

Little fish, little fish,
Swim out to me.
I want to catch you
Without a hook.

What shall I use for bait,
Little fish, little fish?
See, the moon is bobbing
Here in the shallows.

Don't hide in the shadows,
Transparent as a minnow;
Let the sun dress you
In cloth of quicksilver.

Little fish, little fish,
What shall be my lure?
I'll dance on the water,
If that will bring you.

Swim into my net,
Little fish, little fish.
Its mesh is of wind.
I will not try to hold you.

Travel in Texafornia

1. *Where to Go, What to See*

Country of push-button patios, air-conditioned swimming pools
     and
Artificial roses, lush paysage
Of computers and freeways, desert
Of man-made Rocky Mountains, state of euphoria,
Confusion, oranges and nuts—

                                                      To view
From the plexiglass bubble-dome of my head the thousand-and-one
Natural objects of its flotsam-and-jetsam landscape—

                                                      To hold
Simultaneously in the mind Notre Dame and
A drugstore that parthenogenetically produced Lana Turner eating
Her sundae, and in the hand
A dozen avocado pears without any pits—

                                                      To believe,
Finally, that it exists—
Is this possible?

2. *History*

When Fra Junípero went back to Mexico with, 'in addition to
     his breviary and his underwear,'
The mother of the sun in his suitcase; when
The missions were mud, and there was silver in the hills; when
     underground
On yeasty oceans of oil thick blisters broke and boiled; when
     the Alamo
Fell to Davy Crockett, half mountain lion, half alligator;
     when little dogie
Skipped to the slaughter, yes, 10-gallon hats and saddles
     studded with turquoise,
That's history.

3. *Principal Products. Industry and Agriculture.*
   Cultural Monuments.

To get to know the people.
To be invited to lunch in somebody's home. Just folks.
        Mr. Cadillac,
Which way to the lost-and-found? I've been mislaid.

4. *The Itinerary. How Distance Equals Romance.*

It's a long way to that country of savage citrus
And mechanical wayside shrines, to where the sweet swell
Of the desert Pacific lures them and lulls them all, old men
        and wives,
Schoolteachers, building contractors, intent as lemmings:
So, thirty years ago, the aunts, setting dauntlessly out in
        a Dodge,
Rolled over the prairie, crested the Rockies, defeated
The desert: the sea! the sea! I hear them calling,
Like old Victrola records, in far-off, tinny
Voices; over the glimmering wine-dark sea
Of thirty years, their siren voices call.

5. *I Imagine Myself There at Dusk, Thinking of Home*

In two dimensions, flat as a paper doll,
Myself parades across an enormous landscape
Of giant shellfish. Low in the long Pacific
Evening, an orange or a lemon

Glows; without heat, two cars
Collide. Palpable shadows stretch
Across the uneasy continent to the other ocean. Dusk
Reverses itself to dawn. The ubiquitous sun,
Star of the west, sinks down, sinks down, sinks down.

In the Junkshop

1. By sticks and rags, by brass, glass, rust,
   By chairs without backs, by hinges
   Without tables, by stoppers
   Without bottles, by everything broken,
   Cropped, bobbed, docked, truncated—
   Dolls' legs and arms, toy carts without wheels—shawls
   That crumble like ash, old reticules, gloves, lids
   Without boxes, shards, crumbs, splinters, by all trash
   And litter, by the departed souls
   Of things, I conjure up
   This woman: she is the vision;

   Do not be afraid, children, she will not hurt you.

   There is nothing she cannot love, her speech is gentle;
   Her arms on the arms of the chair are at peace, like a statue's;
   Her eyes turn inward, she has the second sight.

   Everything comes to her, she grasps at nothing.
   Among fragments of gloom, forgetfulness, waste, and the
       unwanted
   The proprietress is enthroned; this is what it is
   To be beautiful; she is whole; there is no thing
   She could not encompass, nothing she could not know.

   Here in the half-dark room she does not wait, but blossoms.

2. There is a man in the picture, a shabby creature
   Puttering in the background among rungless chairs.
   Pay attention to him. He is First Assistant Magician.
   From out of his toothless mouth a thread of tune
   Dribbles like ectoplasm. His little eyes
   Scuttle like mice, some feet above the floor.

What are you doing here, Apollo Smintheus,
King of the mice? You keep your distance, cats.

3. Communion with objects. Things natural and unnatural.
A man murdered by his furniture.
Fresh from the factory, things say, Need me! Need me!
Everything Must Go.

4. In these dull rooms, so difficult of access, so crammed
With objects used up, broken, supplanted, the furniture
Of Limbo, surely the tables turn,
The sleepers speak. Materializations,
Mysterious messages, rappings, answers to questions,
Solutions to problems of the heart, how
To get on in business, regain health and vigor,
Are not uncommon. "If you're so smart, why
Aren't you rich?" Under the weight of these things,
She is the witch, she is the sibyl, she is the voice.
Priestess of Limbo, with your attendant god,
Unriddle the open secret. Tell us how
To clean them, scour them, scrape them, reshape them,
Remake them. Sell us our past again. Let their past free us
From all in our own that is foul, fusty, shabby, and sour.
Exorcise them! Evict them, into our daylight apartments;
Let nothing be hidden, in the clear light from the north.

For Picasso

I have seen what God can do
With the backbone of a fish, how he played
The music of the spheres on those pale, pearly bones.

Sweet order, buried in the sweet flesh,
Let us pray to you. In the translucence of your whiteness,
In the symmetry of your severely elegant fillets,
In the pliability of your substance,
In the sharpness of your angles and the thorniness of your points,
Let us read a good word, o chaste hieroglyphic,
And let it not, being a fishbone, stick in our throats.

The Oracle at St. Louis

Many moons ago I lived. Again I
come—Patience Worth my name.

The perfume of God's garden is wasted on jackals
The fruit of the tree is stamped in the mud
The star shines, steadfast as an angel, in the sky,
    but no eye is lifted up

The god spoke
Not through the lips of a starlet with Hollywood dentures
And pencilled lips and eyebrows; not even
In a childish babble (signifying innocence). No.
The oracle
Was sluttish and unwashed, probably stank. Also,
All that smoke made everyone cough.

Similarly,
In St. Louis in 1913,
'A semi-literate housewife'
Wrote a series of astonishing works
Dictated to her by a 17th century spirit.

My light comes from the moon.

TWO

The Moon Tree

Old Wives' Tale

Moon, mother of vegetables,
When I sat by the pond of the hares
(Being as yet unborn),
I worshipped by pulsing of gills.
Swaddled, by rattles and bells.

When I was a daughter, by ribbons
Of watered silk, and ribbons
Of smoke, and by grey ashes (as the mountain ash
Preserves against witchcraft).

When I was a woman
I knew there was no safe place
Above, or on, or underneath the earth;
And I even envied the dead.
Which was blasphemy.

When I grew old, my beads
Were amber, and warded off evil.
We are all gypsies, sister,
Telling what we do not know.

Because the Three Moirai Have Become the Three Maries, or Faith, Hope, and Charity

Moon that is a cow, being horned like her,
Moon that is a panther, rapacious of light,
Moon that is a she-bear, a lioness,
Three-headed hound of the moon,
Moon-muse, mother, fountain that rises and falls,
Your daughters do not forget you.
You make their weather. Their blood
Ebbs and flows like the tides you make.

On one cusp of your crescent, the Black Virgin,
Veiled compassionate daughter, mediatrix, lover of men;
The Mermaid on the other, false siren, half fish,
Half woman, born of the sea, sea-water in
Her veins, salty and cold as the sea; they are
Your children, these two; forget them not.

I standing on your crescent, madonna, moon,
Old woman that never dies, being perpetually
Renewed, made nothing again, made small again,
Waxing again, going through it all over again,
I would lift up my song, bark, howl, bay to you;
I would say to you, remember me, beloved 3-headed nurse,
I have swallowed your milk, you wiped me and wrapped me;
Beautiful motherly monster, watch over me still.

The Moon Garden

Nothing grows there. Cold.
Dry. The sky's a pool.
Glows. Phosphorescent fish.
Stones. Sand.
Color all bleached out. Bones.

This tree grows
Like the antlers of a deer. This shrub
Resembles coral.
Gravel like grass: smooth.
What moves
Trembles as candle flame
Is troubled by the breeze, or blows
Like fine sand through the interstices
Of a fossil skeleton. Shapes, in the pale
Half-moonlight, keep their clarity.
Edge to edge,
Keep definitions.

The Moon Tree

Soft as a worm, its root
Burrows toward the center of the earth
    Show me the root

With trellis and torches
Its branches are lighted up
    Show me the branches

Its leaves quiver
Dark fish in a still pond
    Show me the leaves

It blooms with warnings and
Messages, paper flowers
    Show me the blossoms

The heart of the holy tree
No man has entered. Here
    Sits the mother, eye of the world;

Her son is the green one.
He is the moonmaker. On the tree
    The round fruit waxeth.

The One-Eyed Bridegroom

I have said I will marry the moon,
Little husband of all women,
The son of the serpent,
The one-eyed bridegroom.

For in the keen edge of his sickle,
In his flood-tide,
In the mirror which is himself,
My secrets are hidden.

I marry you in the name of Eve,
Who is the face within the circle;
In the sign of the hare with three legs.
Our first daughter will be a cat, and see in the dark.

Eye of the world, milky, blind, inward-turning eye,
In the dark of the moon, behold! the spouse.

The Moon as a Slice of Watermelon: Lullabye

I'll speak in the beetle's voice
Wear
Worm's armor
Doze halfway
Like the hummingbird
Between rainbow and mulberry

Or I'll be dog lop-eared
Hangdog
Bitch chained in the yard twitching
Under the spell of a sleep that draws back
The lips from the muzzle
Cat I'll be cat
Who made a map of the moon

So in the great ringed round
Eye
Of the duck who flies
Southward over these barrens
Or scavenges crusts and rinds
At the rims of ponds
All can be encompassed
All will sleep sound

Home

Yo no soy yo, y mi casa no es mi casa

Expatriate from the moon, I remember
No craters and deserts, nothing
Like what they imagine.

Their telescopes lie.
Their cameras show false images.

They have dismantled
The apartments of my childhood;
The furniture
Is stored in a warehouse, or sold.

Some of the buildings
Have been pulled down,
And in the old neighborhood
Even the configuration of the streets
Is different.

And yet I had a glimpse
Of myself just now,
Going into that doorway.

I thought it was home.

THREE

Grandfather

My grandfather dealt
In scissors and steel;
Now he is a ghost,
But his knives are real.

He left his wife
Three daughters, a son;
They sharpened their wits
On her whetstone.

I don't know where
Those two lie in the ground,
But a real knife cut
Jack's beanstalk down,

And left us here
With dark coming on,
In the giant's country,
Alone, alone.

The Madman

At first, he wondered why he should be spared;
Observed, of all the windows, none was barred,
And every door swung open at a word.

The garden welcomed him; the angel's sword
Flowered before his eyes like Aaron's rod;
At first he wondered that he should be spared.

The beasts had grown so tame they hardly stirred;
The wall uncoiled its length without a guard
Where every door swung open at a word,

And trees bowed low to offer all they had.
The woman swore he was her only lord
Although, of all the windows, none was barred.

He called it Eden (but it was the world),
And so, until it was too late, ignored
The lucid glass that sealed the windows hard;

No longer troubled to pronounce the word.
But at the end, when towering clouds hurled
Boomerangs at him, and the thunder roared

At him one terrible and final chord,
He knew at last that he had not been spared,
Ran screaming from the mirror, and was mad.

Lines for My Grandmother's Grave

When she died at last it was in the fall of the year
Outside her window the children going to school
Passed with long shadows morning and afternoon

Boys in the street ran at football and piled their sweaters
Carelessly on the curb the little girls
Minded the solemn baby in his carriage

In the lingering twilight of the apartment houses
Out of those sour backyards no harvest was gathered
But the bins in the supermarket were full of fruit

Far off on the avenue behind the windows
Of the expensive shops all the lifelike figures
Scented and hatted and furred achieved nirvana

Enclosed in eternal ennui they are immortal

Darkness fell early but night was slow in coming
Where they bolstered her in a chair no saccharine vision
Of lavender-fragrant old age in a cloudy halo

In the tight little bedroom of the nursing-home
Where the scrubbing-brush fought against the smell of mortality
She ruled like the empress of an angry island

Pitching her voice against those who refused to hear her
The joints of her fingers swelled with indignation
She tossed on the ocean of her recollections

Long ago in the rocking boat she came with the eldest
Over the edge of the world because she had to
And had to forget the world behind her back

Because only tomorrow she knew is truly immortal

Her children's children were never real to her
When they brought her presents although she tried to thank them
And her husband these forty years or more in the grave

Had turned to a fiction although he had left her
A houseful of chattering strangers to worry over
Grieving to think of the endless parade of tomorrows

Marching along toward unspecified destinations
In the gathering dusk anticipating night
Perpetually at bay outside the windows

After she died they found she had written poems
In the language of her girlhood that they could not read
And were partly ashamed of to think that she had not forgotten

But they marked her grave with a stone which is immortal

Witness for the Prosecution

I have left tracks behind. The birthday candle
Is not blown out. The lock of baby hair
Sticks in the full-grown throat.
No real storm ever shook the dollhouse walls;
Somewhere the school report
Is docketed with the receipted bills.

How can we possibly explain away
That testimony, never innocent?
The crooked "I," unnoticed in the typing,
The matchbook cover with its pencilled message
Forgotten on a table in the bar,
In ambush, were conspiring for betrayal.

The important letter, torn across and crumpled,
Was evidence, left for the maid's accounting
One morning in the transient hotel.
Detritus of a thousand separate nights
Awaits the sweeper in the terminals
After the travellers have taken flight.

Nothing is trivial. Yesterday is now.
No closet can contain its skeleton;
The secret scar is tattooed on the forehead.
Today is littered with the spoor of living
Where love, intimidated by the public buildings,
Commits a nuisance in the crowded street.

Outside the door the indifferent judge is waiting
(There is a key for even the cleverest lock).
The dead are not exempt. The poet's quarrel
At midnight with his wife, is documented.
The wreath laid on the coffin will unravel
Baring a human stench, not flower-scented.

No artifact remains anonymous.
The objects that we own can turn on us,
And that accusing moment in the box
Destroy the virtuous fiction of our boasts,
Without machinery of words or fists.
Hear this: the prosecution never rests.

The View from Black's Hill

The plots of ground inhabit the countryside;
Stone walls divide the hill's sweet slope
That once was whole; the web of invading fences

Is spreading; stakes and string
Make fine distinctions between the grass-blades,
And every house inhabits a plot of ground.

Whether of brick or stucco or wooden siding,
The houses have taken possession, have worked transformations;
Lawn and backyard enclose them and surround them,

And on every rooftop the television antennae
Stretch spidery arms to ward off loneliness.
The woman inhabits the house; its rooms reproach her;

The sunlight is waiting; even the dust
Retreats from her still, out of habit, under the bed;
But she struggles no more than the fly sucked dry by the spider

In a corner she overlooked, now her eyesight is failing.
She inhabits herself. In her ailing old woman's body,
Veins, arteries, nerves, bone, most intricate web,

She is the spider that, loving or not loving,
Spins the days out because she must, and around her
The house encloses her, and the plot of ground

Encloses the house, and the web of roads and walls
Encloses the plot of ground, and the television antennae
Blossom on every rooftop, making the sign of the cross.

Collage for Christmas: Mexico City

> "We did not know . . . whether what appeared before us was
> real, for . . . in the lake . . . in front of us stood the great City
> of Mexico."
>
> —*Bernal Diaz*

The only realist in these
Romantic streets is sun. He goes
Down, even, with a difference
(Of emphasis, perhaps), where the
Round earth is tipped a quarter-turn
Away. Pastiche metropolis,
Collage of crazy walls that sink
Wells in the stone; here maps mislead.
(All maps mislead.) The pole-star sways
Above the sagging roofs, and round
As if the moon hung on a tower,
Church clocks anticipate the hour.

The midnight rooster, treading his
Hens in the unswept patios
In the deep center of the maze,
Announces nothing. 'Many stones,
In modern times, lack virtues.' Through
The swaddling night, a violence
Utters earliest cries. Half-built
Houses loom mountainous; beyond,
Where mountains ring the plain, they seem
Bodiless as the rooster.

                    When
Picasso stuck visiting cards
On canvas, 'as exceptionally thick
Patches of white,' all Paris shook;
The early bell, its solid sound,
Textures the sleeping square, and starts

An earthquake rumbling underground
Deep in the stone. The whispering
Voices under the pillow tell
Tales of the fierce dead gods, who set
These stones on water, and so built
Thick patches of the real.

                         Along
Treacherous pavements at the crack
Of day, the black-shawled figures take
The first steps of their pilgrimage,
On conscientious, calloused feet
Walking the waters of the lake.

Sor Juana Inés de la Cruz

"God make me a saint."

They named a street for her. These days
It looks (a dust-hole alley in
Perpetual clamor of the yards)
Through sullen window-sockets on
Its own corruption; powder of her bones
Commingles, in some other place,
With bones of foolish virgins.

                             Some
Of them, perhaps, were granted sanctity,
Stand in the portals of cathedrals, hold
An anchor or a harp, a wheel or grill—
Implements of their art or martyrdom;
She, never.

                Drank the thin air of the high
Plains, gave her learning to the poor,
Died of the plague. The changeling nun,
Christ's bastard bride, she strove
Within the labyrinth of love;
Dissected dreams, until the cold
Light sprouted visions on the wall;
And on the pyramid she built
Laid, finally, her smoking heart.

Who is the saint? The one who gives
Alms, or the one who takes them?

                          This
Town is the beggars' haven. Strays
In the public square, like effigies of shame
They ply their shameless trade; and all the time
And space we have is mirrored in their eyes.

Life in Mexico: A Gloss

1. *The Indian Chapel*

There's nothing here for scientific man:
Rubble, some orange peelings in
The dust, a drift of trash; no shred
Or shard from which to reconstruct
The passion that these people act
With paper spears in hand, the head
Crowned with real thorns.

                   Grey as imagined ghosts
Dust rises at the heels of scientists
Who raise no living anguish from
The body of this death.

               More than
A century ago, in a dark room
In wintry Boston, Prescott made
A friend of darkness, till he saw
Great cities rise from savage lakes,
And saw the virgins of the Emperor
Making of feathers marvellous brocades,
And saw before his eyes the grand
Processions of the priests and kings, although
They all were dust, and he himself was blind.

Why do I call to mind the artisan
Who made for Martin, King of Aragon,
A book of hours with painted cherubim
Whose wings are scarlet and viridian?
His actual eye could never see them so
In Catalonia, where no angels flew,
But his essential vision glows
Bright as he painted it, and his grey lord,

Forgotten in the ghostly retinue
Of mediaeval kings, appears
Illuminated by his book of hours.

2. *The People*

Madame Calderón de la Barca, née Fanny Inglis,
the author of "Life in Mexico," accompanied her husband,
the Spanish Minister to Mexico, on his mission to
that republic in 1839.

Coming the long way round, two months
Tossed in the packet-boat, becalmed
Eleven days in sight of Vera Cruz;
Then savage landscapes, where the children even
Babbled in strange tongues; where bandits' heads
Were nailed as warning in the road;
She, caring not at all to live
Among people whose bite is venomous,
Likely she knew some qualms. And then
Came to the half-barbaric city; found
Satin and velvet gowns, mantillas of
Finest lace, 'a monotony
Of diamond earrings,' gold chains wound
Three times around the neck, touching the knees,
And, on every finger, two diamond rings
'Like little watches.'
                              She remained
A lady among savages, explored
Dark continents in the metropolis;
Transplanted elegance could not
Disguise the wilderness.

And how
Precariously we live in these streets
Filled with the sound of building, when a witch
Lives in the shadow of the steeple.

The faithful cross themselves, and touch
The charm against the evil eye
Hung round the baby's neck, for they
Are neighbors to dark powers. They recognize
The ancient enemy in modern dress,
The tempter through his rational disguise.

3.   *The Dogs*

The heathen emperors died well;
Moctezuma was brave. He went
Knowing the wind was full of knives, aware
Mountains might crush his shade before
He found the river bleakly flowing;
After him, too, his heirs, with names
Difficult to pronounce: they died
Bravely; the Spaniards in their histories
Testify to it. Squat red dogs of clay
Accompanied their going.

Every night
After the mountains crush the sun
Between their jaws, the dogs begin
A strident concert in the town;
Parched, pinched, choleric, gnawing on
Shadows of their own bones, their snarls,
Silent by day, are rendered visible
In sawtooth silhouette; 'a cry

Rendered plastic'; the 'I'
Whose desperation has become a shriek.

Tamayo painted them, with three blue bones
Arranged in rhythmic sequence (knowing
Colors and forms can carry barbs, and hook
Deep in the mind like cactus spines in the foot
Of a man or dog). The darkness howls
The music of despair, and the hungry jaws
Fasten on nothing. Grinning up
From subterranean sepulchres
The clay dogs of the dead kings turn
Their glutted bellies to the sun.

For the Second of November, Next Year

in memory of Colin Bowden

At one remove from actualities
Of plates stacked in the sink, or soiled
Laundry, it is possible to hear
Taxicabs prowling the boulevard of the lions.

Because the city where you lived is built
Upon a lake, sightless fish swim perhaps
Through the arcades on the street of the republic.
—No one has seen them. Truth, done up

As a beggar-woman with one leg, or in
A pearl-grey homburg, as a gentleman,
Jostled you at the entrance to the bar;
You did not recognize him. What

Were the fountains whispering to the gladioli?
Is there a prophet who can read
The future in the plateglass windows of
The fashionable shops? Or interpret

The voice of doom in the horns of taxicabs?
The season does not change, but hangs
On in eternal spring, at one
Remove from actualities. The green

Of leaves and lawns announces no rebirth;
The sweet delirium of the fountains grows
Tedious, and the flower scents become
So painfully heavy and burdensome

They cannot be sustained by that thin air;
Until the final somber mountain looms
Far down the avenue of the palms,
Warning and beckoning. It was always there,

Though no one spoke of it. The breeze
That makes this smoke writhe wraithlike, and that steals
The dry bouquet from this tumbler of wine,
Blows from that mountain. It will never cease.

FOUR

The Idea of a Hero

Four Unromantic Portraits

1. *Madame Blanchard: Woodcut*

"The hero can prove what he is only by dying."—*Edith Hamilton*

Whatever spectacle the crowd came for
They were not disappointed when,
'Small, ugly, nervous,'
She ascended into Heaven in
A rain of gold. Antiphonal
To their polite applause, the ballast spilled
Glistening, earthward; Madame sailed
Serenely in her gondola
Slung from the great balloon.
                              And then
Up from that sea of faces welled
A murmur like the sea's, the gasp,
The soft release, of wonder at
Her fiery arabesques across the air
—Not understanding what they saw
Until too late: balloon and gondola
Alight, and angels all around
Exploding bright, disguised as Bengal flares—

A cynic wrote: she was a shrew,
Petulant, full of specious fears,
Who sought the Empyrean to
Elude the landlord and the dun.

An unknown artist, who was probably
Not there, outlined her unavoidable,
Final dramatic moment: like
A comet, Madame flashed above
The Paris roofs; then fell and broke her neck.

2. *Arthur Rimbaud: Drypoint*

Discarding the exotic face, forked tongue,
And cloven hooves, Rimbaud put on
The apron of reality to play
Grocer, but unsuccessfully.

When innocently once upon a time
He'd planned imaginary crime,
Just so the literal police,
Taking his fictional for real,
Arrested him and put him in a cell.

3. *Earl Denman: Photograph*

"Who then can be saved?"—*Matt:* 19:25

In an age dedicated to success,
Gentlemen, I present
Earl Denman, destined to spectacular
Failure.
         Under a waning star
He drew his first breath of dissent.

His photograph, clipped, British, and moustached,
Gaunt with self-pity, eyes us unabashed,
Repeating, 'There is something pitiable
About our age.'
              Once, and again,
He challenged Everest and lost;
A tiny, ineffectual

David, who can no longer still
The giant's boast.

He teaches us by example how
To avoid becoming a hero. Never he,
Only his balaclava cap
Ever achieved the mountaintop;
Presented by him to his Sherpa guide,
It rode to triumph on the fellow's head.

4. *Billy the Kid: Stereopticon Slide*

Here are two images, distinct
Down to the diamond stickpin, that will not
Merge: Billy, is this a joke
Like the one you played on Grant to win your bet?
Or a game of frontier patience, you, concealed,
Within these pictures of yourself, the twin
Sides of your coin, in ambush like the time
You dropped Hindman and Brady in the road?

The lefthand likeness shows a bucktoothed runt,
Less than man-size, nevertheless the dude,
Strangely familiar; in the morning paper
They posed a gang of you in black windbreakers,
Sideburns, ducktail haircuts, come
From everywhere, driven like you, betrayed
Like you, by the force that drove them, small again
Like you, slouching near Beaver Smith's saloon,
Squinting into the sun.

But in
The picture on the right, the swagger and

Swashbuckle boldness you put on
With the carnation in the dark lapel,
Fit like your skin. 'Handsome, amiable,
Courageous,' knight-errant of youth,
You ride the ranges of romance
Stirrup to stirrup with your myth.

The double images persist.
No effort of the eye or brain
Wrenches into focus, superimposes
One on the other, so as to cancel out
The inconsistencies of sight and seen.
Somewhere in fact or legend, reality
Cranes furtively around the livery barn
Where Billy waited for the sheriff's men.

The Idea of a Hero

NELSON

1. *The Question*

> 'I wonder, child,' said the old lady when she saw him, 'That hunger and fear did not drive you home.'
> 'Fear! Grandmamma,' replied the future hero, 'I never saw fear; what is it?'
>
> —Southey's *Life of Nelson*

Slack times in the hero-factory. O
For the good old andsoforth, the durable
Article: Lord Nelson, for example, who survived
Being a 10-days'-wonder in the music-halls
And had it all his own way at the end:
Going in full regalia, medals and ribbons
Gleaming in the below-decks twilight, bang-bang
Of cannonry above, fireworks in the rigging, everything.

Even the beginning was classic. Motherless,
A boy at sea; voyages
To the north, to the Indies, undreamt-of
Continents, drawing-rooms, romantic attachments,
Battles; the disappearance of Uncle, the suitable marriage;
Then the connubial letter: 'One hundred and ten days
I have been actually engaged against the enemy;
They have not done me justice.'

O, statues, salutes, 'augmentations to the armorial ensign,'
Perpetually in the future! Meanwhile, daily,
With 'scarcely any intermission of pain day and night,'
To face the enemy afresh, at sea, on shore;—
O noble tedium. O glorious gesture
Rehearsed so often in a darkened house.

What counts is the finale. Let it come
With a loud noise, the proper insignia
Pinned on above the heart, that steadfast target,
And with time for a final word. The public funeral
And public monument follow; the family
Will be granted several incomes and estates.

Palmam qui meruit ferat.

2. *The Voyages*

> The captain reprimanded him sternly . . . and desired to know what
> motive he could have had for hunting a bear.
> 'Sir,' said he . . . 'I wished to kill the bear that I might carry the skin to
> my father.'

Of the first voyage, it is possible to imagine
Enormous encrustations of pale green ice
Festooning the black ice mountains, a skyfull of
Hard white clouds—and,
Near the horizon, a curious brightness—
'No insect was to be seen . . . nor any species
Of reptile, not even the common
Earthworm.' A glassy void
On which the intrepid explorers, keeping
Their difficult balance, must somehow skate.

—The princess, atop the glass mountain, has been changed
Into a bear; the problem remains
The same: Father
Is not impressed.

Of the second voyage, chills,
Fevers, mysterious ills, endless, insomniac
Nights, like the dark night of the soul:

'Well, then, I will be a hero, and, confiding in
Providence, brave every danger.' Siege, rains, disease,
Despair—there is no locale
For that voyage, it is everywhere.

The oceans are full of monsters, the islands submerge
Without warning—the signs in the sky:
In these latitudes, all are ominous.

—Father, at home,
Portly, irascible, is changed
Into a bear. The problem
Remains.

There was another voyage,
Over the dimpled sea to Naples, soft
Winds, flowery scents, and siren-song—
Now in a Paradise of pillows, how
Fitting to be so sweetly soothed . . . 'Come here,
For God's sake, my dear friend, and repose
The few wearied limbs you have left.' Again, and again,
He steered across the fragrant waves
On that same voyage, which never was the same
After the first time.

—Now he in turn
Becomes the dancing bear.
The court, unwinking, waits
His clumsy tumble.

3. *The Battle*

'Tell the surgeon to make haste and get his instruments. I know
I must lose my right arm; so the sooner it is off the better.'

Maybe, like a statue of doubtful
Provenance (but old), the hero grows
Grander by diminution: Goliath
Succumbed to a pebble. Likewise, the Beast
Must have his head cut off before he is transformed,
Made handsome, powerful, and wedded to Beauty.

                                        What then,
On the other hand, of Samson? For O, the risks are great.

The half-man, susceptible, puny, plagued by ills,
Can use the sightless eye (sees visions), the invisible arm,
And so dispose the missing parts that the whole
Is greater than before: so he becomes
Half-god.

Then, is the battle
Over, or only beginning?

                           Fêtes, flowery barges, diamonds,
Sweet Emma 'looking out the softest pillows'—
The stern voice is not deceived: 'It is a country
Of fiddlers and poets, whores and scoundrels.'

                                 And Emma,
Whose portrait on his cabin wall must be turned
Away, before every battle, under what dark banner
Did Beauty surrender to such lovers—
Her lord, the gentle knight, his day long past—her love,
This shrinking hero? Lop
His limbs off, one by one.
The battle will end when all are gone.

4. *The Victory*

'If we succeed, what will the world say?'

They must have hated him, the gross
Bourgeois, gossips, midshipmen, in secret; his own
Man sent him a coffin, carpentered
Out of a shattered mainmast, with pious wishes
That the date of its use be distant.

—And how they thronged
The streets, for his victories and his funeral—
Their victories, and Nelson's funeral. To be
A hero to valets. To be one of them,
Raised to the nth degree. And even then
They'd hate him.
                            Envy, greed,
Malice—all the petty vices
Covet his gifts, his medals, and his lady.
After his death, of course, things change. 'Posterity
Will do me justice.'
                            Surely
'An excessive love of glory'
Is no handicap to the epic man:
Anticipating his apotheosis, taking fire
By spontaneous combustion, he leaps astride
His own triumphal funeral pyre;
The world, well lost at last, can but admire.

MAXIMILIAN

1. *José Blasio*

In the golden age of the Valley of Mexico Quetzalcoatl embarked in his
wizard skiff for the unknown islands; but the people believed that he
would come again. They believed it still when the Spaniards came; some
of them, even, when Maximilian came, took him to be their god; tossed
flowers under the wheels of the imperial coach; burned incense; sang
the ancient hymns.

I think I always loved him. Before
He came to my country, riding on the sea,
Godlike, bearded, white-skinned, I must have loved
The idea of him, the legendary god. Later,
I chose my sovereign.

There is nothing I have forgotten. I can tell you
The clothes he wore, the wines he drank;
I know his favorite dishes, horses, visitors;
That first half-year, we gave more than a hundred
Balls and receptions; we commissioned seven
Portraits by seven painters; the bill alone
For spirits topped a hundred thousand (one
Must show oneself a king).

                    But later on
Among the echoing chambers, he was always
Cold, in the upland chill, so we built a palace,
La Casa del Olvido, in the valley.
Who can forget, being Emperor? They tracked
Him there, his fears; his lady pined
And paled; the others deserted
To bolder leaders; I stayed behind,
Drew up his documents, arranged his assignations,
As if nothing had happened, as if his fate

Had not set out already from the north,
Wearing a black coat, riding in a black
Carriage, black eyes hard as obsidian.
We three stayed on: myself, his Indian
Mistress, and the fat professor,
Yet could not comfort him or keep him safe.

When he went with the soldiers to the Hill of Bells
He made me envoy to the Holy City.
There in the terrible labyrinth I found
The Empress, mad; the Holy Father, blind;
While I ran errands among the fountains
They killed him.
That is what they call history.

2. *Duologue in the Castle of Bouchout*

" 'Pay no attention, Madame, if one talks nonsense,' Carlota was over-
heard saying to herself, 'Yes, Madame, one is old, one is stupid, one is
mad . . . the madwoman is still living . . . Death would be a catastrophe,
Madame, which would come not suddenly, but little by little.' "

Sometimes in this grey weather, surrounded by mirrors,
It seems to one, Madame, that the devil has triumphed.
One saw him face to face, three times in Paris;
Each time he wept. But that was long ago.

—I say he wept, and three times he denied me—

Old crone, blasphemous hag, my sweet familiar,
Gibbering in the glass, the others all
All have forsaken one. One is alone,
Yes, old, yes, mad, Madame. And yet they tell one
One had a husband, emperor or king;
If one remembers right, one shared a throne
Atop a heap of gold.

—Madness, I say,
A great marriage, and murder. Palaces,
Gems, power, treason, and a tomb of mirrors—

And you, old witch, to hobble at one's side,
Crazy and crippled, until beauty, youth,
And all the outward signs of what one is
Appear in this uncertain light to fade . . .

How long these afternoons are, and how cold!
There's thunder on the plain; one grows uneasy
Knowing oneself alone among the dead;

—The other, they have killed him; in the glass
Murder and madness; I watched five empires fall
Splintering like mirrors—

                nonsense, Madame,
One babbles nonsense, for one is not gay;
Something is happening; there is no singing;
It was a dreadful journey, down to Vera Cruz;
The devil travelled with us in the carriage
Even to the Holy City. No one saw.
They tell one, one was beautiful, and reigned
Long, long ago, as in a children's tale;
One cannot tell;

             —They say that girl is mad;
And everything is dead, and I am dead—

One lives among echoes and reflections. When
The wind changes direction, one might take
That rustling of the leaves in the castle park
For the crackle of flame, and think oneself in hell.

3. *Monologue of a Singular Man: Gral. Miguel López*

It was reported that when Maximilian and Carlota made their first entry into Mexico City they were escorted on horseback by the same General López who later betrayed him: a mercenary 'with charming manners and a reputation for treachery.'

Halfway across the capital the street
Of the ultimate indignity is busy, like any street.
The one they called the Emperor is dead
Like any man; his lady
Jabbers in Belgium, mindless as a monkey.
        What is it
That makes a hero? Where you or I
See ships upon the ocean, the hero sees himself
Borne on the immaculate flood.
       I am a plain man, rode
For three years in processions, wore my gold
Braid, medals, ribbons; saluted, bowed,
Slept in a palace; but I am no hero.
Above the beleaguered city I saw the hill,
I saw the ready rifles. I tried to save him
From being a hero. I did not need their gold;
He would have given more, and the rascally Father,
His sly confessor, would have shriven my soul.

I tried to save him, gave him
The papers and the key; any man,
Seeing the squads march out and back
Fumbling and sweaty under the single eye
Of the sun, on the Hill of Bells, would know
What was to come.

      They tell of him
How long ago, in Caserta, in his own world,
He dreamed he would unsheathe the golden sword

73

Of the dead kings, his people, and slay the beast
Ravening on the empire and in his breast.

Now he is clay, having fathered nothing;
Leaving behind him neither throne nor son;
In the capital there is no monument;
The people do not mourn; the widow accuses
Him, in her madness; so history is stitched up
Out of a sleazy fabric.

           Where the firing squad
Lifts unimpassioned guns, the hero sees
Himself upon the hill between two thieves
Without blasphemy, in the pure light of his intention.

Cold as two sapphires his sightless eyes accused them
At the final indignity, when butchers despoiled his body.
The mortifying flesh, in robes of ceremony,
Sailed backward across the ocean.

                 I never stood
On that hill where he fell beside the little generals.
They tell me he was brave. Being a hero
Is a public job. They say I am a coward.

4. *Princess Salm-Salm*

"What counts in America is success. Everything else is mere poetic twaddle and waste of money."

—King Leopold of Belgium, in a letter to Maximilian and Carlota written on his deathbed

Finally, those who remained by his side, with the exception of the Generals Miramón and Mejía, who were executed with him, were cheap adventurers, avaricious self-seekers, petty plotters, and traitors. Among them were Prince Salm-Salm and his wife, a former circus performer in the United States, who tried to get Maximilian to escape, disguising himself by shaving off his beard.

In those days we were all highnesses, majesties,
Excellencies, honorables, graces; I myself,
So help me! was a princess—since
That rogue Salm-Salm, whose ring I wore,
Called himself prince . . .

              In those days, before
The tents were struck for good and the show closed down,
We had our moments. We were not abashed
By the extravagant gesture: To the Emperor,
Chasing death through flaming hoops to prove his blood,
We shouted, Encore!

            But I'll make confession:
Not one of us stood up to be shot down
At the grand finale, when the man in black
Cracked his long whip; we disappeared, instead,
So many puppets in a conjuring trick.

They say that half the kings of Europe sent
For a pardon to Juárez—later, of course;
He had his triumph first, the Indian,
Riding in his black carriage and black coat,

Prim as a clerk, along the boulevards
Of the capital. We were not there to see it.

By good prince Jesus, what a crew we were!
Scoundrels and self-seekers: Fischer, the renegade
Priest, with a talent for intrigue; and the "Tiger
Of Tacubaya," who feared nothing helpless, but who saved
His miserable skin in a stranger's grave;
Salm, soldier of fortune; the traitor López, dead
Of a mad dog's bite; and I was there,
Offered my honor as a sacrifice,
Or ransom, rather—but there were no takers.

And then it ended, like a matinée
At the circus. While still the audience
Is shuffling through the sawdust to the gate,
Tightrope performers, clowns, and acrobats
Put off sequins and spangles to resume
The face of every day,
So when they mingle with the homeward crowd
Nobody notices, or thinks them odd.

We disappeared into the crowd like them. (Who'd recognize
Excellency or prince through the disguise
Of our real selves?)

                    These days
I seldom think about the Emperor.
He had no self to hide in, so he died.

   5. *The House of Forgetfulness*

Nothing of splendor remains; under the jungle,
Sprung pavement, fallen beams; the old foundations

Gaping like graves; and granny, wrinkled
As a fungus, monstrous luxuriance flowering among vines;
Telling her days like beads, seeing,
Twining among branches, the giant butterflies
Pale as the souls of the dead.

She's real, though, dozing in the garden; once
Before her ignorant eyes a company
Posed in the authentic robes of tragedy.
One might believe her old eyes see them still,
Or does she dream? The Emperor,
Halfway disguised as any rural lover,
Embraces, in tableau, the gardener's daughter.
A white moth, signifying virtue, hangs
Above the couple.

        In the second scene,
Comfortless on the terrace goes
The somber shadow of a Queen;
Childless and fatherless, already she
Mourns in the endless brilliance endlessly.

Now the Professor comes, hiding in his coat
His life-destroying apparatus: nets
In which he'll catch the winged and fragile things,
Prey of his clumsiness; in a bottle, sweet
And deadly poison; pins that will impale
Them, finally, upon his wall;
He bobs so comically down the walk
Under his big umbrella, who could take
Science seriously?

        In the fourth tableau,
See how the Gardener's Daughter weeps and weeps.

The melancholy Queen has sailed away;
The Emperor is catching butterflies,
Careless of one already in his net;
Wiser than they in ancient auguries,
The Gardener's Girl already has by heart
Her own last speeches and her final scene.

All this the watcher, in her ignorance,
Saw, did not see; not understanding how
Reality could imitate a play;
How could she understand these actors were
True prototypes, heroes and heroines
Mistaking life for legend?

                    Years
Afterward, mumbling toothless gums, crouched
Among their extravagant ruins, she said
Only, the emperor was grand,
The empress sad, the stout professor droll,
The gardener's girl not even beautiful,
But that she'd heard that all of them were dead.

She is the fact, the old woman hunched in the garden, remembering or
not remembering Maximilian's fountains and terraces and the personages
of his retinue; as for him, sentimental princeling, gentle, irresolute,
proud, obstinate, innocent, not even his ghost paces the ruined vistas.
He marched northward with his mercenaries, but the soldiers of Juárez
shot him, while Carlota was locked, in her madness, in the Belgian castle
of Bouchout. History will have none of the botany professor, like a giant
mushroom under his yellow umbrella—as he is described by the young
Blasio, the Emperor's secretary—; and the Indian girl, the gardener's
daughter, died, so they say, in childbed. Nothing remains but the legend
of their ill-timed magnificence in the palace with 1,100 windows in the
capital, or in the castle atop a basalt crag . . .
                                        'At one end of the grand
salon . . . there had been erected a throne covered with crimson velvet
and the empress wore yellow silk, with emeralds and diamonds . . .'

T. E. LAWRENCE

I.

Nobody's man and boy. Appearances
Are everything: five foot three
Gains a foot under the outlandish
Robes flowing like marble. Levitates. Gold
(Reality) like a slice of the sun
Beaten into a halo, worn
Over a fox's grin. In a drawing-room
Made of sand. Carpets and hangings.
Ceremony. The rough raw youths
Woven into a garland. Sees himself
Beauty and beast; becomes
Monument of himself, turns into stone,
And bows before it.
                    Then,
Willful iconoclast, shatters
God (his own image), self, crawls back
Into the sand (dust), all unmanned,
A pebble, grain, mote, speck, to be unseen,
Unsuspect. Still the sun uncovers
And sets him dancing in its dusty beam,
Preposterous dervish, tranced and doomed
To howl and hop before an empty throne.

2.

Death, you old eremite,
Weathered like a pillar—
Once let the undecipherable,

Mysterious syllable burst from my lips
In uncouth, unimaginable glory
Before they fill my mouth with sand.

3.

Like the wind, what he did could always be observed:
Riding across the desert, blowing up railways,
Breaching Damascus, standing at the right hand
Of savage desert sheiks, ambassadors, generals,
Affixing signatures, inditing documents,
'Backing into the limelight'—even that
They could see. Even humiliations,
Tortures, and private agonies. But never
The man. Was that his secret?
To have so honed away
The merely personal, that all that stays
Is the pure act?

They never found him out. Never.
Was there a man beneath the robes?
The statue—was it hollow at the core?
When they closed their eyes, did he vanish?
Had they created him, or he them? Scholars,
They parsed his verbs, not his noun.

SAINT-EXUPERY

1.

No briefings. No experts, statistics, charts
Of the prevailing winds.
No food in capsules,

Collapsible life-rafts. No flares.
Nobody checks
The equipment (faulty) or takes his pulse.
Not even the press
Records the moment when he launches himself
Once more into treacherous air;
And nobody asks
Why he should want to, or dare to, or do it at all.

For example, New York to Tierra del Fuego.
He's off.
Third landing, he forgets to check the fuel.
They warn him (with gestures): the runway is too short,
The plane too heavy.
Crash.
Bandages.
Celebrations
When he returns to Paris still alive,
Singing and drinking, bravos, healths, till dawn.

Alternatively, Paris to Saigon.
He takes two thermos bottles and a friend,
Detects the leak over the Mediterranean.
A second start.
Primed with bad omens, flies lost and wild;
Thinking he sees the coast, makes for a lighthouse.
Crash.
On a desert plateau, the friends congratulate
Themselves: miraculous to be alive. Paris
Sings, drinks, toasts, celebrates.

You know, Saint-Ex was right? Returning home
After unimaginable hazards, that's the thing,
Not mere success in dreary undertakings.

Your health, old Pique la Lune.
Go thumb your nose
Down all eternity, at man, at moon:
The hero is, not does.

2.
Think of Odysseus, seedy travelling man;
He would have flunked his navigation test,
And none of his adventures would have been,
With proper training, briefings, and the rest.

3.
He was not really old. But sat
Like an old man, in gloomy drawing-rooms
Made for old men, doing what old men do
(While the green bird-boys flew in the blue sky),
Grounded, earthbound, a heavy magus
'Watching Vesuvius erupt, reading Kafka, playing chess'—
Naples, Algiers: 'a stupid room, like a cell'—
Dealing out the cards, listening
To his own insides. Waiting. Even the women
Were someplace else, in far-off cloudy cities.

No flags, no trumpets. The old brave band
Scattered, or dead, or middle-aged. The war
Sapping his juices, like hypochondria.

4.
Where in the files is that green plant that grew
Out of his open wound? I think it festers.

All the old rusty wreckage of his youth
Strewn over Africa and the savage mountains
Of South America: I think it is his monument.

The moment when they pushed his plane out of the sky
Into the wine-dark Mediterranean: that is what he meant
When he said, 'I am master of my own ceremonial.'